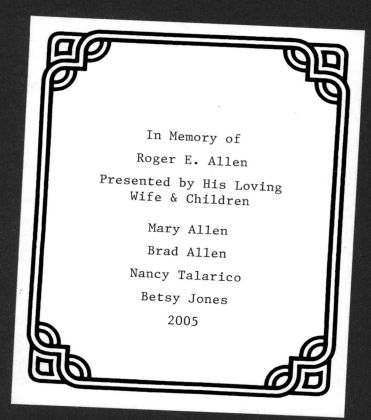

In Memory of

Roger E. Allen

Presented by His Loving
Wife & Children

Mary Allen

Brad Allen

Nancy Talarico

Betsy Jones

2005

Our
New England

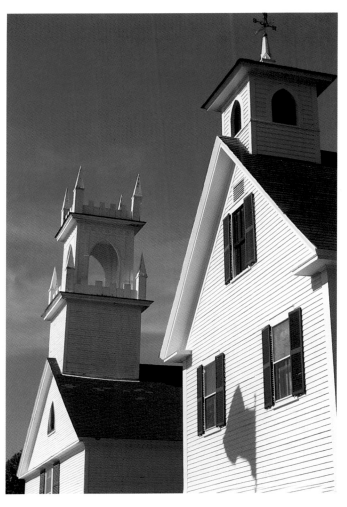

Voyageur Press

04   05   06   07   08   5   4   3   2   1

MPL   LB

Library of Congress Cataloging-in-Publication Data
Our New England.
    p. cm.
  ISBN 0-89658-635-9 (hardcover)
  1. New England—Pictorial works. I. Voyageur Press.
  F5.O95 2004
  974'.022'2—dc22

              2003019314

Distributed in Canada by Raincoast Books,
9050 Shaughnessy Street, Vancouver, B.C. V6P 6E5

Published by Voyageur Press, Inc.
123 North Second Street, P.O. Box 338,
Stillwater, MN 55082 U.S.A.
651-430-2210, fax 651-430-2211
books@voyageurpress.com
www.voyageurpress.com

Educators, fundraisers, premium and gift buyers, publicists, and marketing managers:
Looking for creative products and new sales ideas? Voyageur Press books are available at special discounts when purchased in quantities, and special editions can be created to your specifications. For details contact the marketing department at 800-888-9653.

Page 1: *East Beach near Quonochontaug, Rhode Island, is one of many beautiful white sand beaches that rim the coast along Block Island Sound. (Photograph © Dianne Dietrich Leis)*

Page 2: *The candy-striped West Quoddy Light, located near Lubec, Maine, has marked a treacherous stretch of coastline known as Quoddy Roads since 1808. (Photograph © Susan Cole Kelly)*

Page 3, top: *Susan and Jay Michaud, a husband and wife team from Marblehead, Massachusetts, have been catching lobster in the waters off the New England Coast for twelve years. (Photograph © 2004 Ulrike Welsch)*

Page 3, bottom: *In Bass Harbor, Maine, which lies in the heart of lobster country, piers piled high with lobster traps are a familiar sight. (Photograph © Tom Till)*

Page 4: *A country store in South Woodstock, Vermont, is the place to find everything from Vermont's famous pure maple syrup to handmade soaps and pottery. (Photograph © Dick Dietrich)*

Page 5, top: *Fall colors set off the Swiftwater Covered Bridge, which spans the Ammonoosuc River in the White Mountains of New Hampshire. (Photograph © Tom Till)*

Page 5, bottom: *Ivy dresses the First Congregational Church of Dalton, Massachusetts, in autumnal hues. (Photograph © Paul Rezendes)*

Title page, main photo: *Fishing boats rest in idyllic New Harbor, Maine, a small fishing community near Brunswick. (Photograph © Dick Dietrich)*

Title page, inset: *A church steeple and a one-room schoolhouse stand stoically side-by-side on the village green in Washington, New Hampshire. (Photograph © 2004 Ulrike Welsch)*

Facing page: *The Lighthouse Museum in the old whaling port of Stonington, Connecticut has been a source of information for visitors interested in maritime history since 1925. (Photograph © Kimberly Grant)*

Right: *Views along the craggy coast in the Otter Cliffs area of Acadia National Park inspire many an artist. (Photograph © Susan Cole Kelly)*

Below: *Bass Harbor Head Light has brightened the rocky coast along the southwest point of Mount Desert Island since 1858. (Photograph © Willard Clay)*

Facing page: *The breathtaking cliffs along Ocean Drive in Acadia National Park represent Maine's coastline at its very best. (Photograph © Paul Rezendes)*

Facing page: *From 1,527 feet, the pink granite summit of Cadillac Mountain in Acadia National Park provides a bird's-eye view of the Atlantic coast. (Photograph © Tom Till)*

Above: *A temporary pool near Schoodic Point in Acadia National Park captures the tranquility of daybreak. (Photograph © Paul Rezendes)*

Left: *Yellow lobster shacks and traps top a pier in Maine's Burnt Coat Harbor, Swans Island. (Photograph © Paul Rezendes)*

Top: *Hand-carved wooden fisherman, buoys, and mini lobster traps are favorite souvenirs from Maine. (Photograph © Kimberly Grant)*

Bottom: *Colorful, wooden lobster buoys decorate a lobster shack near Round Pond. (Photograph © Keith Baum/ BaumsAway Stock Photography)*

Facing page, top: *The bustling tourist hub of Bar Harbor is a great place to shop for souvenirs or enjoy fresh seafood. (Photograph © Jerry and Marcy Monkman/ EcoPhotography.com)*

Facing page, bottom: *Whale watching tours depart daily from the Bar Harbor marina. (Photograph © Susan Cole Kelly)*

Above: *Finback whales migrate north in the cool Atlantic waters off the coast of Bar Harbor. (Photograph © Susan Cole Kelly)*

Left: *The sun rises on the coastal town of Camden, a popular tourist destination during the summer months. (Photograph © Susan Cole Kelly)*

Above: *Atlantic puffins are common along the Maine coast. (Photograph © Jerry and Marcy Monkman/ EcoPhotography.com)*

Facing page: *The charming old seaport town of Wiscasset is home to eclectic shops, art galleries, and historic Victorian homes. (Photograph © Susan Cole Kelly)*

Above: *Giant puppets wind down the streets of Old Port during Portland's Old Port Festival parade. (Photograph © Susan Cole Kelly)*

Right: *The first rays of morning sun strike the Portland Observatory and other buildings perched on the hill that overlooks Portland Harbor. (Photograph © Susan Cole Kelly)*

Below: *The Public Market in Portland's historic Old Port is a favorite place to buy local seafood, produce, and baked goods. (Photograph © Susan Cole Kelly)*

Facing page: *A mother and daughter shop for bargains at a boutique on Exchange Street in Old Port, a revitalized neighborhood filled with restaurants, art galleries, and shops. (Photograph © Susan Cole Kelly)*

A group of friends canoe Maine's Allagash Wilderness Waterway, a chain of lakes and rivers that run north from Baxter State Park. (Photograph © Paul Rezendes)

Above: *The Hemlock Covered Bridge has provided safe passage over the Saco River near Fryeburg since 1857. (Photograph © Willard Clay)*

Facing page: *In Grafton Notch State Park, the Bear River twists and turns over Screw Auger Falls. (Photograph © Willard Clay)*

Page 28, top: *A bull moose, Maine's official state animal, cools off in Daicey Pond, Baxter State Park. (Photograph © Susan Cole Kelly)*

Page 28, bottom: *Mount Katahdin reflects in Sandy Stream Pond, Baxter State Park. Katahdin, the highest point in Maine, also marks the end of the Appalachian Trail. (Photograph © Paul Rezendes)*

Page 29: *Katahdin Stream Falls cascades over a granite cliff in four steps, dropping a total of eighty-one feet. (Photograph © Willard Clay)*

Above: *Wild mushrooms stake their claim among birch twigs and fallen leaves in White Mountain National Forest, New Hampshire. (Photograph © Willard Clay)*

Right: *In Fraconia Notch State Park, the Pemigewasset River has worn a pathway through a granite base to create several small waterfalls. (Photograph © Dick Dietrich)*

Facing page, top: *Verdant Long Beech ferns blanket the forest floor of the Waterville Valley in White Mountain National Forest, New Hampshire. (Photograph © Jerry and Marcy Monkman/EcoPhotography.com)*

Facing page, bottom: *The white mark on this tree along the Ethan Pond Trail in New Hampshire identifies the pathway as part of the Appalachian Trail system. (Photograph © Jerry and Marcy Monkman/EcoPhotography.com)*

Above: *The Balsams resort is the main attraction at Dixville Notch in the White Mountains of New Hampshire. (Photograph © 2004 Ulrike Welsch)*

Left: *Mount Monadnock provides the backdrop for this serene setting near Jaffrey, New Hampshire. (Photograph © Paul Rezendes)*

Above: *Bald eagles can be seen soaring with the wind currents above rivers, lakes, and coastline throughout New England. (Photograph © George Wuerthner)*

Above: *The Cornish-Windsor Covered Bridge spans the Connecticut River, providing a sheltered passage between Cornish, New Hampshire, and Windsor, Vermont. (Photograph © Tom Till)*

Facing page: *The autumn sun sets on the picturesque village of Stark, New Hampshire. (Photograph © Susan Cole Kelly)*

Right: *One way to ascend the 6,288-foot Mount Washington in New Hampshire's White Mountains is to board the Cog Railway, which has been hauling tourists to the top since 1869. (Photograph © Paul Rezendes)*

Above: *Mount Washington Hotel has been a famous landmark in the White Mountains since 1902. (Photograph © Paul Rezendes)*

Facing page: *Hikers scale the beautiful but treacherous Mount Washington. (Photograph © 2004 Ulrike Welsch)*

Facing page: *Freshly fallen snow frosts evergreens along the Swift River in New Hampshire's White Mountain National Forest. (Photograph © Paul Rezendes)*

Above: *Conditions couldn't be more perfect for cross-country skiing on this winter's day near the Wentworth Covered Bridge in Jackson, New Hampshire. (Photograph © Dianne Dietrich Leis)*

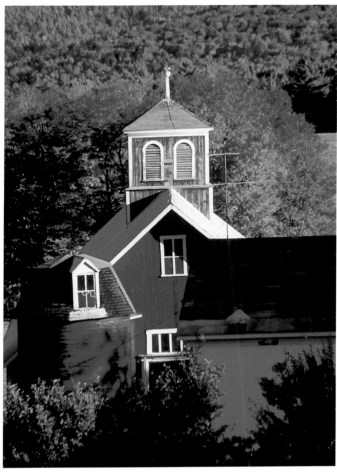

Page 42: *Strawbery Banke on Portsmouth Harbor, established in 1623, is the third-oldest colonial settlement in the United States. (Photograph © Susan Cole Kelly)*

Page 43: *The North Church is one of many nineteenth-century buildings in central Portsmouth. (Photograph © Susan Cole Kelly)*

Left: *The village green in the small town of Norwich, Vermont, glows in the splendor of fall color. (Photograph © Dick Dietrich)*

Above: *This quintessential New England barn and silo in the sleepy town of Barnet, Vermont, appears to blend in with its rural surroundings. (Photograph © Susan Cole Kelly)*

Above: *Old wicker rockers beckon from the front porch of a country inn in Grafton Village, Vermont. (Photograph © Tom Till)*

Facing page, top: *The old-fashioned general store is alive and well in the tiny villages of Vermont's Northeast Kingdom. (Photograph © Susan Cole Kelly)*

Facing page, bottom: *A band concert on the town common in Grafton entertains townspeople on a lazy Sunday afternoon. (Photograph © Susan Cole Kelly)*

Below: *As the snow melts in the Vermont countryside, maple-sugaring buckets are a common sight. (Photograph © Susan Cole Kelly)*

Above: *Vermonters at Harlow's Sugar House in Putney talk as they wait for the sap to cook down. (Photograph © Susan Cole Kelly)*

Right: *Many a sugar house on the back roads of Vermont, including Spring Brook Sugar House in South Woodstock, has real maple syrup for sale. (Photograph © Susan Cole Kelly)*

Smuggler's Notch got its name during the early 1800s when Vermonters smuggled goods into the country from Canada during a trade embargo. (Photograph © Susan Cole Kelly)

The old stone mill in North Bennington, Vermont was built by blacksmith Stephen Whipple in 1823. (Photograph © Dick Dietrich)

Above: *The Natural Arch of Stone is located on private property in the Green Mountains near Warren, Vermont. (Photograph © Tom Till)*

Above: *Moss and ferns cover the granite rocks around this waterfall on a tributary of the New Haven River in the Green Mountains. (Photograph © Jerry and Marcy Monkman/ EcoPhotography.com)*

Facing page: *Hikers pause to enjoy the view while on their way to Mount Mansfield at Underhill State Park, Vermont. (Photograph © George Wuerthner)*

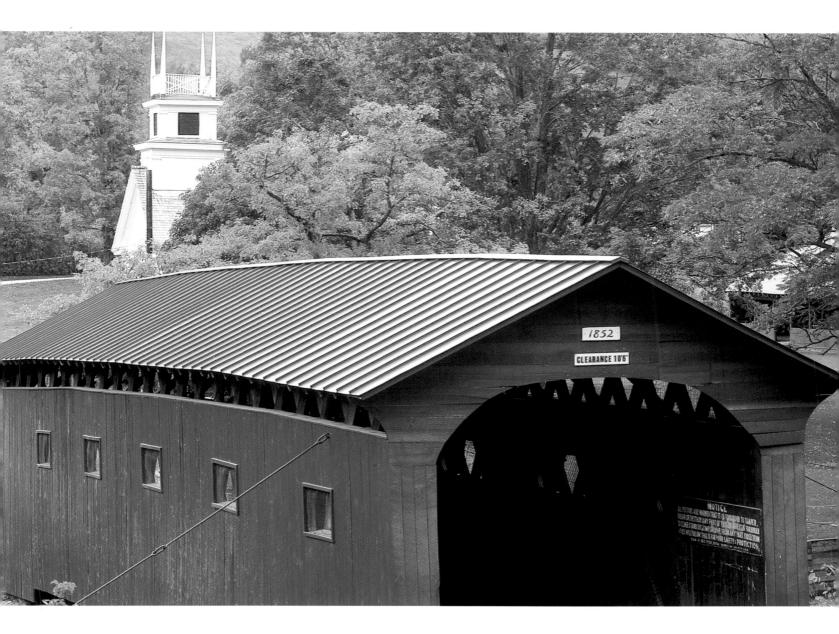

Page 54, top: *The Hall Covered Bridge, which spans the Saxtons River, was built in 1870. (Photograph © Tom Till)*

Page 55, top: *Middlebury's Pulp Mill Covered Bridge, built in 1808, is the oldest in Vermont.(Photograph © Tom Till)*

Pages 54 and 55, bottom: *One of many covered bridges in Vermont, this bridge over the West River in Dummerston was originally built in 1872 and replaced in 1998. (Photograph © Paul Rezendes)*

Facing page: *The Old Bennington Cemetery behind the Old First Congregational Church (1762) is the site of Robert Frost's grave. (Photograph © Susan Cole Kelly)*

Above: *The West Arlington Covered Bridge, built in 1852, spans the Batten Kill River near Norman Rockwell's Arlington home. (Photograph © Tom Till)*

Right: *Shoppers look for bargains at the flea market held each year at the Chester, Vermont, Harvest Festival. (Photograph © Susan Cole Kelly)*

Below: *Cows are part of the quintessential Vermont landscape. These Hereford cows lounge in a grassy field near Newport. (Photograph © Susan Cole Kelly)*

For one weekend in June each year, hot air balloon enthusiasts descend on the charming town of Quechee in central Vermont for the Quechee Balloon Festival and Craft Fair. (Photograph © Susan Cole Kelly)

Above: *The round red barn is but one of the thirty-seven buildings preserved and on display at the eclectic Shelburne Museum, home to a collection of American folk art, fine art, tools, artifacts, and architecture. (Photograph © Susan Cole Kelly)*

Facing page: *The gold dome of the state capitol building in Montpelier brilliantly reflects the light of the sun. (Photograph © Susan Cole Kelly)*

Hartwell Tavern, part of Minute Man Historical Park in Concord, Massachusetts, was an important stop along the Battle Road during the Revolutionary War. (Photograph © George Wuerthner)

Left: *Although calm and tranquil under a layer of freshly fallen snow, the Old North Bridge in Concord was the site of the first battle of the Revolutionary War. (Photograph © Tom Till)*

Below: *A drum and fife choir marches through the streets of Concord during the town's annual Patriot's Day parade. (Photograph © Dianne Dietrich Leis)*

Facing page: *The statue of Roger Conant, the man who founded Salem, Massachusetts, in 1629, stands tall beside the Salem Witch Museum. (Photograph © Susan Cole Kelly)*

Above: *Author Nathaniel Hawthorne brought Salem's House of the Seven Gables into the limelight with his novel of the same name. (Photograph © Susan Cole Kelly)*

Right: *Quaint shops line the streets of downtown Stockbridge in the Berkshires, home of Norman Rockwell for more than twenty years.(Photograph © Susan Cole Kelly)*

Bellow: *Wagon rides through the Berkshire Botanical Garden are popular with children during the Stockbridge harvest festival. (Photograph © Susan Cole Kelly)*

Farmers harvest ripened cranberries, Massachusetts's main crop, in September and October. (Photograph © Ulrike Welsch)

Above: *During the 1930s, Sir Henry Hudson Kitson, the sculptor who created the Lexington "Minuteman," designed this studio in the small Berkshire town of Tyringham. Today the English-style cottage houses a museum and an art gallery. (Photograph © Susan Cole Kelly)*

Right: *The quartzite cliff face of Monument Mountain towers above the surrounding tree-covered Berkshire hills. (Photograph © Paul Rezendes)*

The rustic yet elegant Keystone Bridge crosses a small stream near the Quabbin Reservoir in central Massachusetts. (Photograph © Paul Rezendes)

Myles Standish State Forest in Southeastern Massachusetts offers camping and miles of hiking, biking, and riding trails. (Photograph © Paul Rezendes)

Left: *A visit to Plimoth Plantation provides visitors with a taste of what it might have been like to live in the original Pilgrim settlement in 1627. (Photograph © Dianne Dietrich Leis)*

Above: *Interpreters dressed in the traditional clothing of the seventeenth century go about their daily chores at the plantation. (Photograph © Susan Cole Kelly)*

Right: *Old Sturbridge Village museum is home to restored nineteenth-century buildings that have been moved from sites all over New England. (Photograph © Susan Cole Kelly)*

Above: *Young women, dressed in nineteenth-century costume, walk the grounds at Sturbridge Village. (Photograph © Susan Cole Kelly)*

The round stone barn, built in 1826 and designed to enable one farmer to feed the entire cow herd at once, is the main attraction at Hancock Shaker Village near Pittsfield, Massachusetts. (Photograph © Susan Cole Kelly)

Facing page: *Towering oak and pine trees shade the weathered boards of the Atlantic White Cedar Swamp Trail near Marconi Station on Cape Cod. (Photograph © Susan Cole Kelly)*

Left: *Cape Cod Light, built in 1857, is the oldest light on the Cape. (Photograph © 2004 Ulrike Welsch)*

Below: *Cape Cod is known for its rolling sand dunes and charming clapboard cottages. (Photograph © Kimberly Grant)*

Right: *Brightly colored, Gothic cottages line the lanes of Oak Bluffs on Martha's Vineyard. (Photograph © Paul Rezendes)*

Left: *A family climbs a steep dune before descending to Philbin Beach, a favorite place to whittle away an afternoon on Martha's Vineyard. (Photograph © Dick Dietrich)*

Below: *Aquinnah Light (previously known as Gay Head Light) marks the beautiful, eroded clay cliffs that define the western shore of Martha's Vineyard. (Photograph © Paul Rezendes)*

Facing page: *Brant Point Light shines as the setting sun casts a pink glow over Nantucket Island, Massachusetts. (Photograph © Paul Rezendes)*

Above: *Old clapboard cottages rim tranquil Nantucket Harbor, once a lively whaling port. (Photograph © Paul Rezendes)*

Annisquam Harbor Light has marked Squam Bar on Cape Ann near Gloucester, Massachusetts, since 1897. (Photograph © Paul Rezendes)

Left: *Leonard Craske's* Gloucester Fisherman *is a tribute to the industry the famous seaport was founded on in 1623. (Photograph © Susan Cole Kelly)*

Below: *A fishing crew unloads the day's catch at a Gloucester pier. (Photograph © 2004 Ulrike Welsch)*

Above: *Colorful boats moored in Rockport Harbor frame the famous red fishing shed in the distance. (Photograph © Susan Cole Kelly)*

Facing page, top: *Seafood lovers line up outside Woodman's Restaurant in Essex to sample delicious steamed lobster and fried clams. (Photograph © 2004 Ulrike Welsch)*

Facing page, bottom: *Digging for clams is a popular pastime among locals and tourists in Essex, Massachusetts. (Photograph © Ulrike Welsch)*

Above: *The U.S.S. Constitution, which earned the nickname "Old Ironsides" during the Revolutionary War because of its ability to withstand repeated cannonball assaults, is decorated in lights for Boston's Fourth of July festivities. (Photograph © Dianne Dietrich Leis)*

Right: *The Tall Ship Parade of Sail, made up of about 100 ships from around the world, enters Boston Harbor each summer. (Photograph © Dianne Dietrich Leis)*

Facing page: *In downtown Boston, the Hancock Building towers over historic Trinity Church. (Photograph © Dick Dietrich)*

Above: *Flowering trees, water features, and flower gardens make Boston Public Garden a much-needed respite from the bustling inner city. (Photograph © Dianne Dietrich Leis)*

Left: *The Old State House, a tall building when it was built in 1713, is now dwarfed by surrounding skyscrapers. (Photograph © George Wuerthner)*

Right: *On Patriot's Day each year, between 15,000 and 20,000 runners line up to run the Boston Marathon, the world's oldest annual 26.2-mile foot race. (Photograph © Ulrike Welsch)*

A women's rowing team competes in the Annual Harvard Rowing Competition on the Charles River in Boston. (Photograph © Dianne Dietrich Leis)

Boston's famous Back Bay neighborhood was created when developers filled a low-lying, swampy area of the city to build more housing. (Photograph © Dianne Dietrich Leis)

Above: *The house of Paul Revere in Boston's North End was where the famous patriot began his fateful midnight ride to Lexington on April 18, 1775. (Photograph © 2004 Ulrike Welsch)*

Left: *Narrow cobblestone streets traverse the hilly terrain of Beacon Hill, one of the oldest and most popular Boston neighborhoods. (Photograph © Susan Cole Kelly)*

Facing page: *It was in the steeple of the Old North Church, built in 1723, that Paul Revere hung a lantern to warn the patriots of the British invasion. (Photograph © Susan Cole Kelly)*

Above: *Quincy Market opened in 1827 as a covered market where shoppers could buy fruits, vegetables, fish, and meat. (Photograph © Susan Cole Kelly)*

Facing page: *At the base of Bunker Hill monument stands a statue of Colonel William Prescott, who led the American troops into battle during the Revolutionary War. (Photograph © 2004 Ulrike Welsch)*

Facing page: *The steeple of the First Congregational Church of Litchfield, established in 1721, peers above brilliant fall foliage. (Photograph © Susan Cole Kelly)*

Above: *The tiny town of Litchfield, Connecticut, is a favorite stop among tourists traveling New England back roads in autumn to view fall colors. (Photograph © Susan Cole Kelly)*

Page 98 and 99, top: *Old stone walls divide estate properties in the Litchfield Hills. (Photograph © Jerry and Marcy Monkman/EcoPhotography.com)*

Page 98, bottom: *In autumn, rolls of harvested hay dot the rolling farm fields of the Litchfield Hills. (Photograph © Susan Cole Kelly)*

Page 99, bottom: *Holstein and Guernsey cows relax on a picturesque farm near Lyme, Connecticut. (Photograph © Paul Rezendes)*

Facing page: *Wild Sweet William, daisies, and Queen Anne's Lace add a splash of color to an old barn near the Housatonic River in Connecticut. (Photograph © Tom Till)*

Above: *An arched fieldstone bridge leads the way to Gillette Castle near East Haddam, Connecticut. William Hooker Gillette, an actor, director, and playwright, built the medieval-style mansion in 1919. (Photograph © Paul Rezendes)*

Facing page: *Chapman Falls, which drops more than sixty feet, is the main attraction at Devil's Hopyard State Park near East Haddam, Connecticut. (Photograph © Tom Till)*

Above: *Hemlocks shade this stretch of the Eightmile River as it flows through Devil's Hopyard State Park. (Photograph © Paul Rezendes)*

Above: *Morgan Point Lighthouse has guided ships along the coast near Noank, Connecticut, since 1831. (Photograph © Paul Rezendes)*

Right: *Sailboats reflect vividly in the calm waters of Old Saybrook's Ferry Point Marina. (Photograph © Paul Rezendes)*

Page 106: *A cigar store Indian stands guard outside a cigar shop in Mystic Seaport, the largest maritime museum in the world. (Photograph © Susan Cole Kelly)*

Page 107: *Mystic Seaport is home to the Charles W. Morgan, a wooden whaling ship built in 1841. (Photograph © Susan Cole Kelly)*

Left: *Yale University was established in Saybrook, Connecticut, in 1701 and moved to New Haven in 1717. (Photograph © Susan Cole Kelly)*

Above: *Lovely Victorian homes face New Haven's Wooster Square. (Photograph © Susan Cole Kelly)*

Facing page: *Bushnell Park in Hartford, Connecticut, provides a stunning view of the gold-capped state capitol building with Corning Fountain. (Photograph © Susan Cole Kelly)*

Above: *Between 1874 and 1891, Mark Twain and his family lived in this Hartford home, known as Nook Farm, built in the Picturesque-Gothic style. (Photograph © Susan Cole Kelly)*

Above: *The historic Fleur-De-Lys Studio, built in 1885, is one of many national historic landmarks in Downtown Providence, Rhode Island. (Photograph © Paul Rezendes)*

Right: *The eighteenth- and nineteenth-century buildings that face Thomas Street in Providence's historic district have been renovated into art galleries and museums. (Photograph © Paul Rezendes)*

Facing page: *The Rhode Island State House tops Constitution Hill in downtown Providence. (Photograph © Paul Rezendes)*

Left: *Providence, once a seventeenth-century seaport, has undergone significant renovation over the past twenty years. (Photograph © Paul Rezendes)*

Bottom: *In the summer months, gondoliers offer rides through Waterplace Park in Providence. (Photograph © Paul Rezendes)*

Above: *A strong summer breeze carries these yachts past the Newport Bridge. (Photograph © Susan Cole Kelly)*

Facing page: *Beavertail Lighthouse marks the waters off the southern tip of Conanicut Island. (Photograph © George Wuerthner)*

Shops, restaurants, and art galleries inhabit the restored buildings of Bowen's Wharf in Newport, Rhode Island. (Photograph © Paul Rezendes)

Facing page: *Newport's famous Cliff Walk trail provides breathtaking coastal views and a peek at historic mansions built at the turn of the century. (Photograph © Paul Rezendes)*

Above: *A family explores tiny tide pools along the Newport coast. (Photograph © Dianne Dietrich Leis)*

Above: *In 1892, William K. Vanderbuilt commissioned architect Richard Morris Hunt to build Marble House on Newport's Bellevue Avenue. (Photograph © Susan Cole Kelly)*

Right: *The Breakers, designed by Hunt in the style of the Italian Renaissance, was the second Vanderbilt mansion to find a home along Newport's Cliff Walk. (Photograph © Paul Rezendes)*

Above: *Clambakes like this one in Bristol, Rhode Island, have been a New England tradition for centuries. (Photograph © Ulrike Welsch)*

Facing page: *The Fourth of July Parade in Bristol is one of the best Independence Day celebrations around. (Photograph © 2004 Ulrike Welsch)*

Above: *Block Island North Light was established on Sandy Point in 1829. The deactivated light is now a public museum. (Photograph © Paul Rezendes)*

Right: *One of the best ways to tour tranquil Block Island, located about twelve miles south of Narragansett Bay, is by bicycle. (Photograph © Susan Cole Kelly)*
Left: *Along Block Island's Beacon Hill*

Road, horses graze in pastures divided by stone walls. (Photograph © Susan Cole Kelly)

Salt marshes, grasslands, and rolling sand dunes make Sachuest Point National Wildlife Refuge a haven for migratory birds. (Photograph © Paul Rezendes)